URSA

Where You DARE Not Go

Dreadful Dwellings

SCARY GHOST TOWNS AND LOST CITIES

by
Natalie Lunis and
Sarah Parvis

Minneapolis, Minnesota

Credits

Cover, © Cavan/Adobe Stock and © ysbrandcosijn/Adobe Stock and © annette shaff/Adobe Stock; 4–5, © Alexey Marakhovets/Adobe Stock and © auremar/Adobe Stock and © Jennifer/Adobe Stock and © agus/Adobe Stock; 6, © Kenzos/Shutterstock; 7TR, © Jim Parkin/Shutterstock; 8, © Jim Sugar/Getty Images; 9TR, © Adam Constanza/Adobe Stock; 10, © FiledIMAGE/iStock photo; 11TR, © Richard Cummins/Alamy Stock Photo; 11B, © Gutyryak_Irina/Adobe Stock; 12, © Tupungato/Shutterstock; 13MR, © Francesco Bonino/Adobe Stock; 13BL, © Massimiliano Marino/Shutterstock; 14, © Cavan-Images/Shutterstock; 15TR, © Public domain/Wikimedia; 15MR, © by-studio/Adobe Stock; 16, © Chris Yaxley/Adobe Stock; 17B, © R Kawka/Alamy Stock Photo; 18, © Sopotnicki/Shutterstock; 19TR, © Nat25alie Jean Ruffing (N. Jean)/Adobe Stock; 19B, © tatui1761/Adobe Stock; 20, © Penguin company/iStock photo; 20MR, © berichard/Wikimedia; 21BR, © Fairfax Media/ Getty Images; 22, © Konstantin L/Adobe Stock; 23TR, © Stock Montage/Getty Images; 24, © Debbie Firkins/Shutterstock; 25MR, © Guillem Lopez/Alamy Stock Photo; 26, © Marcelo Rabelo/Adobe Stock; 27TR, © Bildagentur-online/Alamy Stock Photo; 27B, © BlackMac/Adobe Stock; 28, © jordi.magrans/Shutterstock; 29TR, © Public domain/Wikimedia; 29BR, © Kanuman/Shutterstock; 30, © RODOLFO CONTRERAS/Alamy Stock Photo; 31MR, © Brigitte/Adobe Stock; 31BL, © GARY DOAK/Alamy Stock Photo; 32, © Aflo Co. Ltd./Alamy Stock Photo; 33TR, © leungchopan/Adobe Stock; 34, © Nikada/iStock photo; 35TR, © Public domain/Wikimedia; 35BR, © AfriramPOE/Shutterstock; 36, © sayilan/Adobe Stock; 37TR, © Mongkolchon/Adobe Stock; 38, © Aleksandar Todorovic/Adobe Stock; 39BR, © Alan/Adobe Stock; 40, © Mikkel Juul Jensen/Science Source; 41TR, © funstarts33/Shutterstock; 42–43, © Triff/Shutterstock

Bearport Publishing Company Product Development Team

Publisher: Jen Jenson; Director of Product Development: Spencer Brinker; Managing Editor: Allison Juda; Editor: Cole Nelson; Associate Editor: Naomi Reich; Associate Editor: Tiana Tran; Designer: Kim Jones; Designer: Kayla Eggert; Designer: Steve Scheluchin; Production Specialist: Owen Hamlin

Statement on Usage of Generative Artificial Intelligence

Bearport Publishing remains committed to publishing high-quality nonfiction books. Therefore, we restrict the use of generative AI to ensure accuracy of all text and visual components pertaining to a book's subject. See BearportPublishing.com for details.

Library of Congress Cataloging-in-Publication Data is available at www.loc.gov or upon request from the publisher.

ISBN: 979-8-89577-092-4 (hardcover)
ISBN: 979-8-89577-209-6 (ebook)

Copyright © 2026 Bearport Publishing Company. All rights reserved. No part of this publication may be reproduced in whole or in part, stored in any retrieval system, or transmitted in any form or by any means, electronic, mechanical, photocopying, recording, or otherwise, without written permission from the publisher. Bearport Publishing is a division of FlutterBee Education Group.

For more information, write to Bearport Publishing, 5357 Penn Avenue South, Minneapolis, MN 55419.

Contents

Abandoned, Ghostly, and Lost 4

The Gold Rush Ghost 6

Mysterious Islands 8

Headless Charlie 10

Going Downhill 12

A Spooky Sheriff 14

Swallowed by the Sea 16

Hidden Homes 18

A Drowned Town Reappears 20

The Lost Colony 22

The City of the Crystal Skull 24

A Violent Volcano 26

Buried in Sand 28

The City Below 30

Built and Then Forgotten 32

Lost Temples of Stone 34

An Ancient Legend Comes True 36

A Haunted Pyramid 38

Searching for a Sunken City 40

A World Full of . . . Dreadful Dwellings 42

Glossary 44

Read More 46

Learn More Online 46

Index 47

Abandoned, Ghostly, and Lost

In a ghost town, the houses are all empty and nobody is in the streets. All you hear is an eerie whisper or the sound of distant animals howling in the night. Where has everybody gone, and could something more sinister be lurking in their absence? And what about the entire cities that have completely vanished? When they are discovered many years later, is it wise to learn the secrets they hold?

The Gold Rush Ghost

BODIE
CALIFORNIA

In 1859, gold was discovered in Bodie, California. Thousands of people soon moved to the area, hoping to get rich quickly. By the 1940s, however, very little gold could still be found in Bodie. With no more work, the miners left, and the town shut down. One person, however, is said to still call Bodie her home.

Bodie, California

Bodie, California, started around 1861 with only 20 gold miners. By 1880, it was home to more than 10,000 people, and with more than 60 saloons, the town was famous for being wild. Robbers, gamblers, and gunfighters lived among miners and store owners. Some say that a murder occurred in the town almost every day.

The J. S. Cain house

Several hundred people also worked in service occupations in Bodie, including a maid for the successful businessman James Stuart Cain. One day, Mrs. Cain fired the maid in a jealous rage, and the maid was so upset that she killed herself. Park rangers in the abandoned town say that her spirit has never left.

One night, a ranger's wife was sleeping at the J. S. Cain house. She suddenly woke, gasping for breath. When she opened her eyes, she saw Cain's maid sitting on top of her. Fighting to get away, the ranger's wife fell off the bed. When she looked up, the ghost was gone.

Is Bodie cursed? After taking objects from the town, such as pebbles or pieces of wood, some visitors have started to have terrible luck. Some had car accidents. Others lost their jobs. Many of these visitors rushed back to Bodie to return the items, hoping to get rid of their bad luck.

Mysterious Islands

NAN MADOL
MICRONESIA

In the middle of the vast Pacific Ocean lies a group of tiny human-made islands surrounded by high walls. Huge, heavy stones were used to build the little islands over a period of hundreds of years, mostly between the 1200s and the 1600s. Later, the islands were abandoned—except for the ghosts who are said to still guard them.

Some of the human-made islands that make up Nan Madol

The ancient city of Nan Madol lies just off the coast of Pohnpei, a natural island that was home to a group of people known as the Saudeleurs. These islanders used log-shaped stones to build a city made up of 92 islets. Around these tiny islands, they built high walls to keep the ocean waves from washing the city away.

The ruins of Nan Madol

Nan Madol was home to the families of powerful chiefs. It was also where priests lived and took care of the tombs where previous chiefs were laid to rest.

Over time, the people of Nan Madol left their city. No one knows exactly why, though some believe it became too difficult to bring fresh food and water to the islands. Even today, few people visit the ruins because they are so hard to reach. According to those who live nearby, the visitors who do manage to reach Nan Madol are in for a shock. That's because ghosts are said to haunt and protect the ruins of the city that was once their home.

It is still unknown how the islanders who built Nan Madol managed to move the heavy stones they used. According to legend, the ancient builders used magic to get the heavy slabs to fly into place.

Headless Charlie

JEROME
ARIZONA

Some miners strike it rich with gold, while others search for silver. Beginning in the 1880s, miners in Jerome, Arizona, found their fortune in copper. More than $500 million worth of the metal was taken from the Jerome mines before they closed in 1953. Was it worth the price paid in miners' lives?

Jerome, Arizona

Mining is a dangerous business. Accidents, fires, explosions, cave-ins, and poisonous gases are common threats. After uncontrollable fires swept through the mining tunnels beneath Jerome in 1918,

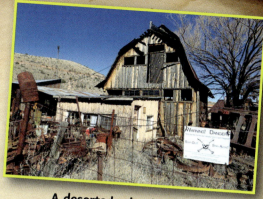

A deserted mine in Jerome

underground mining was stopped. Instead, dynamite was used to blast open the ground to get the metal.

During World War II (1939–1945), the miners of Jerome were very busy. The United States needed lots of copper to make engines, planes, ships, and wires. After the war, however, the need for copper dropped, and the town slowly died. By the time Jerome's last copper mine closed in 1953, only 50 people were left in the city.

Today, the miles of abandoned tunnels that run under the town can be spooky. They are said to be haunted by Headless Charlie. Charlie was a miner whose head was chopped off in a terrible accident. His body was never found. Maybe his spirit never left the dusty tunnels.

The Inn at Jerome is said to be home to a ghostly cat. Workers have felt it brush past them in the halls and have heard its meow. Some even say the cat leaves the print of its body on beds where it sleeps.

Going Downhill

CRACO
ITALY

The sturdy stone houses of Craco, Italy, were built high on a hill to keep people safe from enemies. Unfortunately, the buildings could not protect the people from the many disasters that would strike the city.

The abandoned city of Craco

The huge tower that marks the highest point in Craco dates back to around 1000 CE. The people who lived there at that time needed the structure to watch for invaders approaching from the surrounding countryside. Over the next 500 years, the town grew, and more buildings filled up the steep hilltop.

Although Craco was not attacked or destroyed by enemies, the town suffered disaster after disaster in the centuries that followed. In 1656, plague swept through, killing hundreds of people. During the 1800s and 1900s, earthquakes and landslides rocked the land. In addition, bad weather conditions often killed the crops in nearby fields. Finally, in 1963, it was decided that the town had become completely unsafe as a result of these natural disasters. All the remaining residents were moved to a nearby valley, and the town was abandoned.

Inside an abandoned church

Although no one lives in the town of Craco any longer, visitors are still allowed to walk in the city's narrow streets and tour its crumbling buildings.

A Spooky Sheriff

BANNACK
MONTANA

From the 1860s to the 1890s, the area west of the Mississippi River was known as the Wild West. Gamblers and criminals lived alongside cowboys and miners in this part of the United States. To keep people safe, the towns needed good sheriffs. It wasn't always easy, however, to tell the good ones from the bad....

Bannack, Montana

In the summer of 1862, gold was found in a creek in Bannack, Montana. A year later, the town had 3,000 people and more crime than it knew how to handle. The townspeople elected newcomer Henry Plummer as their sheriff. No one knew he had recently been in jail for murder.

Henry Plummer

After Plummer became sheriff, people were still being robbed. In fact, crime in the town got worse. In just a few months, more than 100 people were murdered. Plummer was accused of being the leader of a gang of criminals. Although he was never proved guilty, Plummer was dragged to the gallows by angry townspeople and hanged in January 1864.

By the 1940s, there was no gold left in Bannack. The few remaining people moved away. Yet Sheriff Plummer's ghost is said to remain. People have seen it lurking among the silent buildings. Is the dead man trying to prove his innocence or cause more trouble?

According to legend, Henry Plummer's grave was robbed around 1900. Two men were said to have stolen his head. They carried it back to the Bank Exchange Saloon. It remained there for several years, until the building burned down.

Swallowed by the Sea

DUNWICH
ENGLAND

At one time, Dunwich, England, was a booming town. Thanks to its seaside location, it was an important port city, naval base, fishing town, and shipbuilding center. Over the years, however, the same sea that had brought so much growth and success also caused most of the town's homes, churches, businesses—and people—to disappear.

The ruins of Dunwich

By 1100, Dunwich had one of the largest populations of all the cities in England. It was the capital of a region known as East Anglia. Then, in January 1286, a giant storm hit. Huge waves washed over a large part of the town and swept it into the sea. More storms followed over the years, along with more destruction. By the early 1900s, most of Dunwich's buildings had been lost to the restless North Sea.

Today, Dunwich is a tiny village. Fewer than 200 people live there. Where there were once more than a dozen churches, there are now only the crumbling ruins of just one. The town's remaining residents, however, are still sometimes reminded of the churches that once stood. They say that church bells can sometimes be heard rising up from beneath the waves.

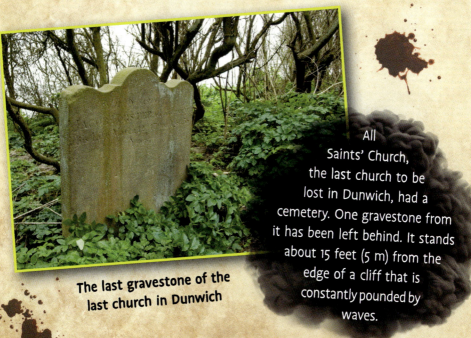

The last gravestone of the last church in Dunwich

All Saints' Church, the last church to be lost in Dunwich, had a cemetery. One gravestone from it has been left behind. It stands about 15 feet (5 m) from the edge of a cliff that is constantly pounded by waves.

Hidden Homes

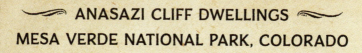

ANASAZI CLIFF DWELLINGS
MESA VERDE NATIONAL PARK, COLORADO

The western part of North America was home to Native Americans long before miners and cowboys moved in. The Anasazi (*ah-nuh-SAH-zee*) were an ancient people who were already living in the American Southwest 2,000 years ago. In the 1100s, they began building homes into the sides of high cliffs. Then suddenly, around 1300, they disappeared. Would anyone ever see their beautiful homes again?

Anasazi cliff dwellings

In 1888, two ranchers in Colorado were looking for cattle that had strayed from the herd. Instead of cows, however, they came upon an eerie sight.

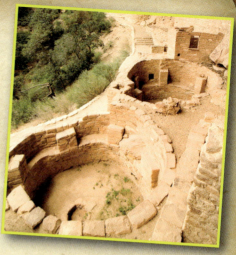

A kiva

Tucked into the cliffs above them were crumbling homes that had been built by the Anasazi. The buildings were made out of sandstone bricks. The most amazing one is called Cliff Palace. It includes more than 200 rooms and 23 underground kivas, or meeting rooms. Spirits of the Anasazi have been seen around the kivas.

At the time the cliff dwellings were discovered, the Anasazi hadn't lived there for more than 500 years. It's possible they left because of drought or warfare with nearby tribes. Whatever the reason for their disappearance, no one lives in the cliffs now except scorpions, rattlesnakes, coyotes—and perhaps spirits from a time long past.

Scientists found more than a thousand broken and burned bones in the Anasazi's abandoned buildings in New Mexico. Many of these bones were from humans. Some believe they belonged to Anasazi victims who were killed and eaten by enemies.

A Drowned Town Reappears

OLD ADAMINABY
AUSTRALIA

Sometimes, cities and towns are lost underwater because of floods or other forces of nature. There are also times, however, when an entire community is deliberately submerged. Such places then become known as drowned towns. One of the most famous—and strangest—of these sunken towns is Old Adaminaby.

The town of Old Adaminaby lies beneath this lake.

An undated photo of Adaminaby

When the water level is normal, trout fishing is a popular activity on the lake that flooded Old Adaminaby.

In 1957, Australians were working on a huge engineering project. Its purpose was to capture water from melting snow to use for the creation of two large lakes. The water in the lakes would then be used to help farmers grow crops and to spin turbines to help produce electricity.

To create one of the lakes, the project's engineers had to flood a town called Adaminaby. They moved some of the town's homes and buildings to nearby dry land and submerged others. At that point, the newly built settlement was named New Adaminaby, and the town at the bottom of the lake became known as Old Adaminaby.

Exactly 50 years later, in 2007, a terrible drought hit. As the lake that had covered Old Adaminaby slowly dried up, houses, trees, trucks, and other parts of the abandoned town slowly reappeared—like ghosts that had come back to haunt the living.

The stairs of St. Mary's Church were revealed after the water level receded.

The Lost Colony

ROANOKE ISLAND
NORTH CAROLINA

In 1587, about 115 English settlers arrived by ship at Roanoke (ROH-uh-nohk) Island. The small island is located off the coast of North Carolina. The settlers hoped to make a new home for themselves there. Within three years, however, all of them would disappear.

A replica of the ship that brought settlers to Roanoke Island

The men, women, and children who reached Roanoke Island were tired and hungry from their long journey. They lacked basic goods, such as food and tools. So, the colony's governor, John White, sailed back to England to get supplies. He left behind his family, including his newborn granddaughter, Virginia.

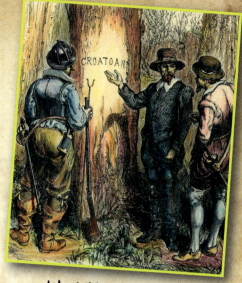

John White discovering the word *Croatoan*

Unfortunately, White was unable to return for several years due to war. He finally arrived at Roanoke for the second time on August 18, 1590—his granddaughter's third birthday. However, the island was deserted. All the houses had been taken down, and not a single person could be found. Only one clue remained. The word *Croatoan* (*kroh*-uh-*TOH*-un) was carved along a fence. It was the name of a local tribe. Yet why it was written there, no one knows.

White returned to England, never discovering what had happened to his family. To this day, the mystery of the lost colony has never been solved.

Sir Richard Grenville, an English explorer, had stopped on Roanoke Island in 1586. He left 15 men there to claim it for England while he gathered more settlers. When John White arrived in 1587, he found the bones of one man, but there was no sign of the others.

The City of the Crystal Skull

LUBAANTUN
BELIZE

More than a thousand years ago, the Mayan people built great cities in a part of the world that is now made up of Mexico, Belize, Guatemala, El Salvador, and Honduras. In the early 1900s, an expert who studied Mayan sites came upon a city that was unlike any he had ever seen before. Was there an object that has supernatural powers there?

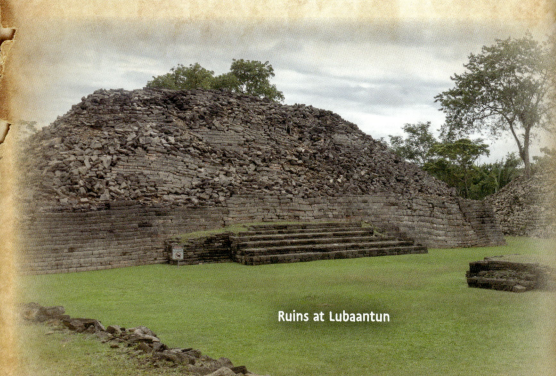

Ruins at Lubaantun

The Maya were great builders. Within their cities were palaces, temples, and pyramids. Usually, these mighty buildings were made up of large rectangular blocks carved from stone and held in place with mortar.

In 1903, a British archaeologist named Thomas Gann heard about a series of ruins in Belize. When he explored them, he was amazed by what he found. The ancient city, called Lubaantun, had eleven large buildings. They were different from other Mayan buildings because they had rounded corners and were built mostly without the use of mortar.

During the 1950s, Lubaantun became known for another unusual find. An English writer named F. A. Mitchell-Hedges claimed he had a life-size crystal skull from the ancient ruins. Both Mitchell-Hedges and his daughter, Anna, claimed that Anna had found the skull in a temple in Lubaantun in the 1920s—although there was no proof that Anna had ever been to the site. Later, Anna would also claim that the skull—which came to be known as the Skull of Doom—had mysterious powers, including the power to bring about a deadly curse.

The Skull of Doom

Several experts who have done scientific tests on the skull have concluded that it was made in modern times and, therefore, could not have actually come from Lubaantun. Still, some people today continue to speak and write about its Mayan origin and its supernatural qualities.

A Violent Volcano

POMPEII
ITALY

How did Pompeii, a busy city of 20,000 people, become a ghost town overnight? It got buried under ash and rocks from the eruption of a massive volcano. The disaster in Pompeii was so swift and deadly that many people didn't even have time to escape. They were simply buried right where they stood.

Pompeii today

On August 24, 79 CE, people in the Roman city of Pompeii felt the earth shake. A huge burst of ash from Mount Vesuvius rose more than 12 miles (19 km) into the air. Nearly 6 inches (15 cm) of fiery rock and ash fell onto the city every hour. The roofs of many homes caved in. Poisonous gas from the volcano filled the air.

Mount Vesuvius erupting over Pompeii

People ran for safety, but many could not escape. About 2,000 people died on that terrible day. The city remained buried under many feet of volcanic debris, untouched and forgotten for more than 1,500 years.

Pompeii was rediscovered in 1748. Since that time, many of the city's buildings and homes have been uncovered. Now, the millions of tourists who visit the city can imagine what life was like before tragedy struck.

A victim of Mount Vesuvius

Over time, the bodies buried by the volcano decayed. Empty spaces in the shapes of the victims were left in the hardened ash. Archaeologists poured plaster into the spaces. When it dried, the hardened plaster looked just like the people of Pompeii at the moment of their deaths.

27

Buried in Sand

KOLMANSKOP
NAMIBIA

Every day, the blazing hot sun of the Namib Desert beats down on a spooky sight. Well-built houses, some with fancy decorations, have sat unused for decades, slowly filling up with desert sand. Where did this grand city come from? And what made its inhabitants vanish, leaving their beautiful homes behind?

Abandoned houses in Kolmanskop

Today, visitors can tour what is left of Kolmanskop during the day. According to some, it's lucky that the abandoned town is closed at night. Why? People claim that after dark, ghosts come out to visit the places where they once lived.

One day in 1908, a worker named Zacharias Lewala was shoveling sand near a railroad track that ran through part of the Namib Desert. He saw something glittering and picked it up to take a closer look. The sparkling object was a diamond.

Zacharias Lewala

Word of the lucky find spread quickly. By 1910, a town had sprung up to provide a home for those who flocked to the area to gather up the precious stones. The town, called Kolmanskop, included not only houses but also a school, hospital, theater, ballroom, and ice factory. Because the company that ran the prospecting operation was German, the buildings were designed to look like those from a well-off German town.

By the 1920s, almost all the diamonds had been removed from the area. At that point, the people who had come to Kolmanskop began to leave, and by 1956, everyone was gone. It wasn't long before sand carried by the desert winds covered the streets. As windows broke and doors blew open, sand also entered the houses and buildings, leaving a knee-deep layer. Now, more than 50 years later, Kolmanskop lies buried by time and the desert.

Inside a home filled with sand

The City Below

MARY KING'S CLOSE
EDINBURGH, SCOTLAND

Mary King's Close was once a crowded neighborhood of narrow alleyways in Edinburgh, Scotland. By the 1600s, the area had become filthy, run-down, and full of disease. City leaders decided to get rid of the dirty neighborhood by building on top of it. Their plan created an eerie underground ghost city.

Mary King's Close

In 1753, builders in Edinburgh, Scotland, knocked down the top stories of the buildings in Mary King's Close. They used the bottom halves of the old buildings to hold up larger, new ones. The alleyways that were once noisy and busy were left below in silence. The empty underground streets were not opened to the public again for more than 200 years.

Today, the most famous resident of Mary King's Close is known simply as Annie. She was a young girl who died from the bubonic plague in 1645. Annie's ghost was first seen by a Japanese psychic in 1992. In one of the tiny underground rooms, the psychic suddenly felt sick. When she tried to leave, she felt someone tug at her leg. She turned to see the ghost of a girl, dressed in rags. Her hair was long and dirty. Since then, other visitors have seen Annie, and many now bring gifts for the lost little girl.

Tour guides have seen shadows in the shapes of humans gliding around Mary King's Close. When the light bulbs in the underground passages burn out, the guides go in pairs to fix them. They are too afraid to go alone.

How many ghosts haunt Mary King's Close?

Built and Then Forgotten

HASHIMA ISLAND
JAPAN

About 9 miles (14 km) off the coast of Japan lies an island called Hashima. Some people call it Battleship Island, since its tall concrete buildings and high seawalls make it look like a giant battleship floating in dark ocean waters. Others call it Ghost Island, because the place is now only a ghost of its former self.

Hashima Island

Today, tourists are allowed to take a ferry and visit Hashima. However, they are allowed to see only part of the island. The crumbling buildings that make up the rest of it are considered dangerous.

Hashima was once one of more than 500 rocky, completely uninhabited islands off Japan's southwestern coast. Then, in the 1890s, a large company called Mitsubishi began a mining project to dig out coal from the seafloor around the island. At first, workers traveled from the Japanese mainland to their jobs by ferry. Later, however, Mitsubishi built huge blocks of apartment buildings on Hashima so workers could live there. By the late 1950s, there were more than 5,000 people on the tiny island—making it one of the most crowded places on Earth.

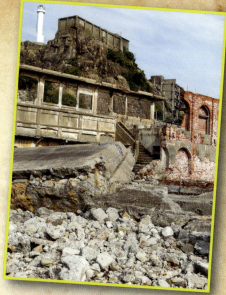

Crumbling buildings on Hashima

Just as the population of Hashima was reaching its peak, oil was becoming Japan's most important energy source. As a result, the demand for coal went down, and so did the amount of mining done from Hashima. Finally, in 1974, the island was shut down and all the people moved away. With no one left to take care of them, buildings and seawalls began crumbling. The only sounds to be heard in a place that was once as crowded as any city in the world were the crashing of waves and the whistling of the wind.

Lost Temples of Stone

ANGKOR
CAMBODIA

The Khmer ruled much of Southeast Asia from the 800s to the 1400s. They built a huge capital city at Angkor, Cambodia. In 1431, the powerful Khmer were defeated by people from Thailand. As a result, they were forced to abandon Angkor. For more than 400 years, the beautiful city remained hidden deep in the jungle.

Angkor, Cambodia

In 1860, French explorer Henri Mouhot stumbled upon the hidden city of Angkor. He was amazed by what he saw. The Khmer had filled their city with huge, beautiful stone temples. One of them, Angkor Wat, is thought to be the largest religious building in the world.

Henri Mouhot

Today, monks often travel to Angkor to pray. They believe that the spirits of people who once lived there remain. Some monks have reported seeing ghosts of princes and princesses walking through the stone halls and courtyards. Perhaps these royal ghosts continue to rule the city of stone.

When a French archaeologist first walked through the newly discovered city of Angkor, he felt as if he was being watched. Terrified, he looked up and saw huge faces looking down at him from all sides. These faces were giant stone sculptures carved into one of the temples.

A carved face in Angkor

An Ancient Legend Comes True

TROY
PRESENT-DAY TURKEY

According to one of the world's most famous legends, there was once a mighty city not far from ancient Greece. High walls wrapped all the way around the city to help defend it from enemies. They proved useless, however, against a deadly trick that was thought up by a clever leader on the enemy side.

The ancient ruins of Troy

Archaeologists studying the site in Turkey think that the seventh layer from the bottom, known as Troy VII, is the walled city destroyed by the Greeks.

The walled city of Troy was made famous by two ancient poets—a Greek named Homer and a Roman named Virgil. Each told about a war between the Greeks and the people of Troy, known as Trojans.

For 10 years, the Greek army surrounded Troy but was unable to enter its walls. Finally, a Greek general named Odysseus had the idea to build a wooden horse so big that a group of warriors could hide inside it. The Greeks built the horse and left it outside the city walls. When the Trojans brought it inside, fighters spilled out and opened the city gates so more of their soldiers could enter. The Greeks then killed most of the people within Troy and burned the city down.

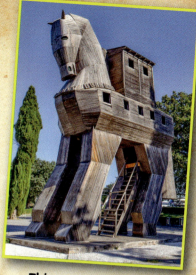

This model shows what the Trojan horse might have looked like.

For a long time, no one knew if Troy had really existed. But in 1870, a German archaeologist named Heinrich Schliemann began digging for the ancient city in a hill in Turkey. Before long, he had uncovered layers of ruins showing that, over time, nine different cities had stood on that spot. Today, experts agree that one was probably the real-life Troy.

A Haunted Pyramid

UXMAL
MEXICO

The Mayan people thrived from 200 CE until 900 CE. In some areas, they remained powerful until the 1500s. These incredible peoples built enormous cities with tall pyramids and beautiful temples—all without using machines or metal tools. So why did their advanced civilization die out?

Uxmal, Mexico

In the early 1500s, the Spanish arrived in Mexico looking for gold. During their search, they killed many of the Mayan people. The Spanish also brought new diseases to the area, such as smallpox. These illnesses spread quickly among the Maya, killing thousands more.

As a result of the Spanish invasion, the incredible cities of the Maya became ghost towns and were often forgotten. Some would not be rediscovered for hundreds of years.

The ancient city of Uxmal (oosh-MAL) is one such ghost town. It is now helping archaeologists learn about the Maya, including their practice of human sacrifice. Atop the stone Pyramid of the Magician in Uxmal, Mayan priests used to sacrifice people to honor their gods. The ghost of one Mayan priest still haunts Uxmal. When he's seen, he is dressed in his ceremonial robe and feathers. Visitors have spotted him atop the stone pyramid as if getting ready for another sacrifice.

To perform their sacrifices, Mayan priests sometimes chopped off the heads of their victims. Other times, they used a stone knife to remove the beating heart from a living person. Then, the priest would throw the body down from the top of the pyramid.

39

Searching for a Sunken City

ATLANTIS
LOCATION UNKNOWN

Was there once a magnificent city filled with people who had an amazing amount of knowledge about building, farming, and sailing—long before the Egyptians, Greeks, and Romans? For more than 2,000 years, many have believed such a place existed, and some have even searched for it.

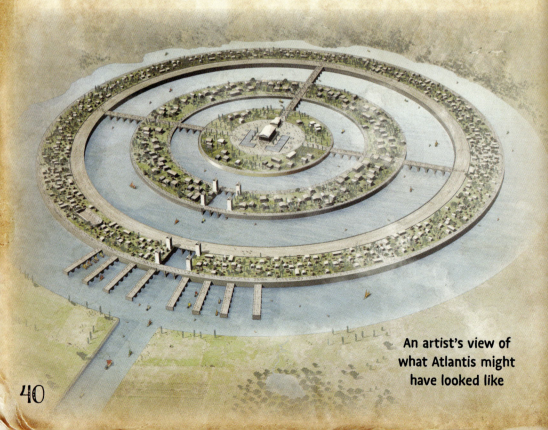

An artist's view of what Atlantis might have looked like

Around 360 BCE, a Greek philosopher named Plato wrote about an island called Atlantis. In the center of the island was a beautiful city that contained a palace, along with temples, statues, fountains, and canals. The people who lived there were not only great builders but also great sailors and traders who traveled all over the world.

A painting of Atlantis under the sea

According to the story, the Atlanteans eventually became greedy and disrespectful. As a result, the Greek gods punished the islanders by causing earthquakes that made the island sink into the sea.

Today, people disagree about Atlantis. To many, it is simply part of a story Plato made up to teach a lesson about how people should live. Others, however, point out that Plato included a great deal of factual information about the island's location. To them, Atlantis is a real city that is lost but will someday be found.

Experts have claimed that clear evidence of Atlantis has been found in various locations, including spots off the coasts of Greece, Italy, and Spain. Many thousands of years ago, all of these places were struck by giant earthquakes or huge tsunamis.

A World Full of . . .

A corrupt sheriff in
Bannack, Montana

Abandoned dwellings in Mesa
Verde National Park, Colorado

A cursed town in
Bodie, California

A lost colony on Roanoke
Island, North Carolina

A headless miner
in Jerome, Arizona

**NORTH
AMERICA**

A haunted pyramid
in Uxmal, Mexico

The Skull of Doom in
Lubaantun, Belize

ATLANTIC
OCEAN

PACIFIC
OCEAN

SOUTH
AMERICA

The lost city of Atlantis—
location unknown

SOUTHERN
OCEAN

Dreadful Dwellings

Glossary

abandoned left empty or no longer used

ancient very old

archaeologist a scientist who learns about people of the past by studying ancient objects, such as old buildings, tools, and pottery

ash tiny volcanic dust made of rocks and minerals

canals narrow stretches of water that are dug across land

close a Scottish word for a narrow alley

colony an area that has been settled by people from another country and is ruled by that country

creek a small stream

criminals people who have broken the law

curse something that brings or causes evil or misfortune

debris scattered pieces of something that has been destroyed

decayed rotted

deserted left empty or alone

drought a long period with little or no rain

dwellings places where people live; homes

eruption the sending out of lava, ash, steam, and gas from a volcano

ferry a boat that takes people from one place to another

fortune a large amount of money

gallows a wooden frame used to hang criminals

human sacrifice killing people as part of a ceremony or as an offering to a god

industry a type of business

innocence being not guilty of a crime or wrongdoing

islets tiny islands

Khmer people born in Cambodia; the Khmer ruled much of Southeast Asia from the 800s to the 1400s

legend a story handed down from long ago that is often based on some facts but cannot be proven true

mining the digging of deep holes or tunnels from which rock or other materials are taken

monks men who have devoted their lives to being part of a religious community

mortar a mixture of sand, limestone, water, and cement put between bricks or stones to hold them together

philosopher a person who thinks and writes about the meaning of life

plague a disease that spreads quickly and often kills many people

plaster a mixture of water and powdered rock that hardens as it dries

port a place where ships load and unload goods

prospecting searching the ground for gold, gems, or other valuable resources

psychic a person said to be able to communicate with the spirits of dead people

ruins what is left of something that has collapsed or been destroyed

sacred holy, religious

saloons places where people can buy and drink alcohol

seawalls walls that are built to keep tides and waves from washing buildings or land into the ocean

settlers people who live and make a home in a new place

sites places or locations

slabs flat, thick pieces of something

spirits supernatural creatures, such as ghosts

submerged covered with water

temples buildings used for religious purposes

tombs graves, rooms, or buildings in which dead bodies are placed

tsunamis giant ocean waves caused by earthquakes or volcanic eruptions

turbines machines that are powered by wind, water, or steam moving through the blades of a wheel to make it spin

Read More

Allen, Judy and Dinah Williams. *Alarming Afterlife: Scary Cemeteries and Graveyards (Where You Dare Not Go).* Minneapolis: Bearport Publishing Company, 2025.

Finn, Peter. *Do Ghosts Exist? (Fact or Fiction?).* New York: Gareth Stevens Publishing, 2022.

Hamilton, Sue L. *The World's Most Ghoulish Ghosts (Xtreme Screams).* Minneapolis: A&D Xtreme, 2022.

Sheen, Barbara. *Ghosts and Spirits (Exploring the Occult).* San Diego: ReferencePoint Press, 2024.

Learn More Online

1. Go to **FactSurfer.com** or scan the QR code below.
2. Enter "**Dreadful Dwellings**" into the search box.
3. Click on the cover of this book to see a list of websites.

Index

Anasazi 18-19
Angkor, Cambodia 34-35, 43
Atlantis 40-42
Bannack, Montana 14-15, 42
Bodie, California 6-7, 42
bubonic plague 31
Cain, James Stuart 7
cliff dwellings 18-19
Cliff Palace 19
Craco, Italy 12-13, 43
crystal skull 25, 42
Dunwich, England 16-17, 43
Gann, Thomas 25
ghost town 4, 26, 39
gold 6-7, 10, 15, 39
Greeks 37, 41
Grenville, Sir Richard 23
Hashima Island 32, 43
Headless Charlie 10-11
Homer 37
Jerome, Arizona 10-11, 42
J. S. Cain house 7
Khmer 34-35
kiva 19
Kolmanskop, Namibia 28-29, 43
Lewala, Zacharias 29
Lubaantun, Belize 24-25, 42
Mary King's Close 30-31
Maya 25, 38-39
Mayan people 24, 38-39
Mesa Verde National Park 18, 42
mining 11

Mitchell-Hedges, Anna 25
Mitchell-Hedges, F. A. 25
Mitsubishi 33
Mouhot, Henri 35
Mount Vesuvius 27
Nan Madol, Micronesia 8-9, 43
New Adaminaby, Australia 21
Odysseus 37
Old Adaminaby, Australia 20-21, 43
plague 13, 31
Plato 41
Plummer, Henry 15
Pompeii, Italy 26-27, 43
Pyramid of the Magician 39
Roanoke Island 22-23, 42
Romans 40
sacrifices 39
Schliemann, Heinrich 37
Troy 36-37, 43
Uxmal, Mexico 38-39, 42
Virgil 37
White, John 23